C

Health promoting schools in Wales
Ms Sue Bowker, Health Promotion Wales, and Ms Sue Allerston, Mid Glamorgan Local Education Authority

Multi-disciplinary involvement in promoting school catering
Ms Susan Stainton, Essex Food Services, Essex County Council

Developing a national policy on food advertising to children
Ms Sue Dibb, National Food Alliance

Discussion and key points from the case studies

Foreword

Food for children: Influencing choice and investing in health derives from a conference organised by the National Forum for Coronary Heart Disease Prevention in 1993. The issues and concerns are not new, however. In 1988 the Forum organised a conference on *Coronary heart disease prevention in school-age children.* One of its conclusions was that, in order to reduce the overall risk of coronary heart disease, healthy eating patterns should be established in childhood. Two Forum developmental projects stemmed from that conference: the *School meals assessment pack* (see page 49) and *Eat your words* (see page 48).

The conference also had much wider repercussions in voicing concerns about children's diets and their health implications, and it made several recommendations for improvement. Many of the organisations represented are beginning to undertake work on children's diets and the health implications.

But children's diets have not improved over the past decade. The many major concerns and influences outlined in this report need to be addressed, and action is needed now.

The national health strategies for England, Scotland, Wales and Northern Ireland provide an opportunity to place these issues on the national agenda.

I hope this report will succeed in raising those concerns among health, medical, educational, consumer and catering bodies as well as government and the food industry, and that it will stimulate ideas for action.

I would like to thank all the members of the Steering Group, and also the British Heart Foundation for funding this important opportunity to identify and discuss the issues of concern about the diets of British school children.

Professor Desmond Julian CBE MD FRCP
Chairman, National Forum for Coronary Heart Disease Prevention

CHAPTER 1

Introduction

Coronary heart disease is the major cause of death in the UK, but there is much scope for reducing the risk. The main known risk factors include smoking, raised blood cholesterol and hypertension. There is little doubt that the disease process begins in childhood: cardiovascular risk factors can be identified in early life, and lifestyles and behaviours which influence cardiovascular risk are learned and begin early.[1] Children continue to eat more than the recommended percentage of energy in their diets from fat and consume less than the recommended amount of fibre. Several studies indicate that there has been no improvement in children's eating habits over the last ten years, with fat consumption at up to 43% of energy.[2]

The Forum focuses in particular on the prevention of coronary heart disease, but the diet of young people is important in many other ways too. Firstly, children need a nutrient-dense diet to meet their requirements for growth and development. Secondly, health-related behaviour and attitudes towards food are established in childhood. Thirdly, while some diet-related diseases manifest themselves in childhood, there is good evidence that the disease process for some diseases of adulthood may start in early life.[2]

The aim of the Forum conference on *Diet and school children* was:

- to contribute to an improvement in the nutritional content of children's diets.

The objectives were:

- to improve knowledge of influences on childhood nutrition
- to stimulate an improvement in provision for healthy eating by children
- to examine ways in which Forum member organisations and other agencies can address children's eating habits as a risk factor for coronary heart disease, and stimulate action.

The UK health strategies recognise that establishing healthy eating patterns remains a challenge, and that a wide variety of agents have a role to play in improving provision, promotion and consumption of healthy food choices.[3] The Forum member organisations include those who specifically address children's health, and health education, and there is a need to combine this expertise with the experience and opportunities presented by those who cater for children. A coordinated approach is widely recognised as the most effective way forward.

Health and education professionals and food producers must work together with government to ensure that children have access to a healthy diet and develop eating habits which will lay the foundations for a healthy future life. There is excellent access to children in a learning environment at school. There is ample opportunity to discuss with them the importance of diet, and provide them with an adequate, well balanced meal through the school catering service. The question this report poses is: 'How can more be made of these opportunities?'

References

1   Sharp I. 1989. *Coronary heart disease prevention in school-age children. Report of a meeting.* London: National Forum for Coronary Heart Disease Prevention.

2   Sharp I. 1992. *Nutritional guidelines for school meals.* London: The Caroline Walker Trust.

3   Department of Health. 1992. *The health of the nation: a strategy for health in England.* London: HMSO.

CHAPTER 2

The National Forum for Coronary Heart Disease Prevention

The National Forum for Coronary Heart Disease Prevention was established in 1983, initially as the National Coordinating Committee for Coronary Heart Disease Prevention, following the Canterbury conference *Action to prevent coronary heart disease.*

Within its aim to contribute to a reduction in coronary heart disease morbidity and mortality in the UK, the Forum has four central objectives:

- to keep under review the activities of member organisations in the field of coronary heart disease prevention and disseminate findings
- to identify areas of consensus, issues of controversy, and needs for action in the field of coronary heart disease prevention
- to facilitate the coordination of activities between interested organisations in the field of coronary heart disease prevention
- to make recommendations where appropriate.

The Forum currently coordinates the work of expert representatives from over 35 national organisations involved in coronary heart disease prevention in the UK, including the health services, professional bodies and voluntary organisations. Members also include several individual experts.

Member organisations of the National Forum for Coronary Heart Disease Prevention

Action on Smoking and Health (ASH)
Anticipatory Care Teams (ACT)
Association of Primary Care Facilitators
British Cardiac Society
British Dietetic Association
British Heart Foundation
British Medical Association
British Nutrition Foundation

British Paediatric Association
Consumers' Association
CORDA
Coronary Prevention Group
Faculty of Public Health Medicine
Family Heart Association
Health Education Authority
Health Education Board for Scotland
Health Promotion Agency for Northern Ireland
Health Promotion Wales
Health Visitors' Association
Institution of Environmental Health Officers
National Association of Governors and Managers
National Association of Health Authorities and Trusts
Northern Ireland Chest, Heart and Stroke Association
Royal College of General Practitioners
Royal College of Nursing
Royal College of Physicians of Edinburgh
Royal College of Physicians of London
Royal College of Surgeons
Royal Institute of Public Health and Hygiene
Royal Pharmaceutical Society of Great Britain
Society of Cardiothoracic Surgeons
Society of Health Education and Health Promotion Specialists
Society of Occupational Medicine
Sports Council
Trades Union Congress

Observers
Department of Health
Department of Health and Social Services, Northern Ireland
Medical Research Council
Ministry of Agriculture, Fisheries and Food
National Consumer Council
Scottish Consumer Council
The Scottish Office, Home and Health Department
Welsh Office

In addition, a number of distinguished experts in the field have individual membership.

CHAPTER 3

The way forward

The following recommendations emerged during the discussions at the conference. Their purpose is to help bring about an improvement in the diets of school children in the UK. This means that children should be eating a diet which contains more bread, cereals and other starchy foods; more fruit and vegetables; and less fat, sugar and salty foods; and which is richer in minerals and vitamins.

The typical diet of school children in the UK is high in fat and sugar, low in fibre (non-starch polysaccharides), low in iron and calcium, and possibly low in folate.

A healthy diet is, of course, vital to children's growth and development. Conversely, the typical unhealthy diet increases the risk of a variety of health problems both in childhood and in later life. As well as affecting children's growth and development, diet in childhood may influence the development of dental disease, constipation and other bowel disorders, nutritional anaemia, obesity and overweight, and may increase the risks, in adulthood, of low bone mass, coronary heart disease, stroke, and some cancers including breast and bowel cancer.

Consequently, healthy eating habits should be started early. For maximum effect, observations and interventions need to take place from early primary school age. Diet-related diseases are often multi-factorial, and other factors such as smoking and physical activity should also be addressed.

Changing dietary patterns is a long-term goal. This time scale should be reflected in the plans of interacting agencies such as government departments, health professionals, educators, caterers, food producers, retailers and consumer groups. Planning implementation to achieve change should be seen as a series of small but successful changes which ultimately add up to a larger impact.

Any strategy to improve children's diet must address children's ability and opportunity to make healthy food choices, as well as initiatives to increase knowledge and understanding. The healthy choices should be the easy choices.

Policy development

NATIONAL POLICY

1   National policies are needed which create an environment where the healthy choices are the easy choices. This could include national nutritional guidelines for school meals and supporting demonstration projects within schools which illustrate healthy eating initiatives.

2   There is a need to address poverty as it affects diet. A national anti-poverty strategy, sensitive to the needs of children, is required. This could include improving awareness of eligibility for benefits, to improve uptake; widened eligibility for benefits for low income groups, eg free school meals; and pricing policies which help reduce the cost of a healthy diet.

National policy creates an environment which shapes children's eating patterns and food choices. There is a need to ensure that the policies of different government departments support rather than undermine the nutrition goals of the national strategies for health.

Information alone is not enough. Making healthy choices the easy choices will help change children's food behaviour. Any national strategy to change eating patterns must include implementation and evaluation as well as target setting. In England, the Nutrition Task Force is currently addressing this area.

More than a quarter of children in the UK live in poverty. Social policy affecting the economic status of the family has a cumulative effect on children's diets. Poverty leads to unhealthy or less healthy food choices through altered budget priorities. There is no financial scope for experimenting with new food choices, and often an inability or lack of opportunity to use a variety of cooking skills or equipment.

COMMON AGRICULTURAL POLICY

3   The government should negotiate to achieve European legislation which makes foods which form part of a healthy diet cheaper and therefore more widely available. European policy should take nutrition and health into account.

The Common Agricultural Policy (CAP) is an agricultural policy, not a nutrition policy. The CAP affects 90% of foods in the UK – maintaining prices or affecting the availability of foods. The CAP currently gives a higher subsidy on full fat dairy products rather than reduced fat products in schools, thus encouraging their use. The CAP could be used to promote the consumption of fruit by, for example, creating a free school fruit scheme to reduce current fruit wastage.

In economic terms, although the current policies may appear to generate financial savings in the short term, the long-term economic costs may increase through health care costs, and lost income through absence from work due to diet-related disease. Nutrition and health need to be considered in decision-making.

ADVERTISING POLICY

4   Advertising regulatory bodies, in consultation with public health and consumer bodies, should negotiate new codes for advertising practice and procedures which better reflect current, nationally agreed nutrition and health guidelines.

5   Guidelines for those who produce and use food and nutrition education resources, which clearly identify those free from promotional bias, should be developed and implemented.

A large proportion of children's pocket money is spent on food and drink. Children also influence their parents' spending on food. Their choice of food products is affected by advertising and promotion. The influence exerted by food advertising to children often undermines healthy eating messages. Over half the new food products launched in the UK in 1990 and aimed at children, were for sugar and chocolate confectionery, soft drinks and snack food. Only 10% of food advertisements aimed at children could be said to encourage a healthy diet.

Food advertising and promotion may be included in material produced for use in classrooms, or sent to schools as educational material. Children may also see food advertising on posters in and around schools, and from many other sources throughout the day.

PROFESSIONAL ORGANISATIONS

6   Professional medical and health organisations, and educational agencies, could use their networks and influence to raise awareness of the problems of children's diets and encourage action at a local and national level.

Professional organisations have only recently begun to take on the message about the poor nutritional quality of children's diets and the long-term health implications. National bodies representing medical, health and education professionals can have an important influence on national policy decisions, and could encourage and enable their members to take action at a local level, by disseminating information and allocating resources. The new national health strategies provide a framework for such action.

LOCAL POLICY

7   Local food and health policy groups should be established to identify
     and take action to achieve improvements in children's diets. Such
     groups should include purchasers and providers of local services, such
     as: community dietitian, director of public health, health promotion
     officer, local education authority officer, representatives from local
     schools, school nurse manager, school medical officer, catering
     manager and environmental health officer.

Healthy alliances will be more successful than isolated actions, in coordinating
local initiatives to achieve change. The health promoting school needs a
supportive environment, if healthy eating patterns are to be sustained throughout the day.

   For example, the nutritional content of average school meal provision in the
area could be assessed using a method such as the Forum's *School meals assessment pack* (see page 49), and the results could be included in the annual report
of every local director of public health, and every local education authority.
School-based monitoring could be done by a teacher, caterer and school governor,
and information about school food included in the school report for parents.

Improvements in schools

HEALTH PROMOTING SCHOOLS

8   Schools should develop and implement a healthy food policy, based on
     up-to-date nutritional guidelines, and covering all food eaten in the
     school environment. This should ensure that the knowledge and
     understanding acquired in the classroom are reinforced through food
     provision in the school. This activity is a task for governors, parents,
     heads, teachers, caterers, and pupils.
9   Participation in the European network of health promoting schools
     should be increased.

A wide range of factors affect children's food choices within the school environment. A school food and nutrition policy can ensure that all of these factors
are giving a consistent message.

   Children spend a total of about 15,000 hours at school between the ages of 5
and 16. The foods they eat at school will form an important part of their diet.
Foods promoted by the hidden curriculum of vending machines, tuckshops and

school meals have an important influence on reinforcing or undermining class-room learning on food, nutrition and health.

Foods other than high fat or high sugar snacks (such as crisps, sweets and soft drinks) should be available to children at breakfast and breaktimes. All vending machines and tuckshops should sell a range of foods including lower fat and lower sugar items, illustrating that snack foods can be part of a healthy diet.

School policies can also be used to affect children's access to foods off the school premises.

CURRICULUM

10 Healthy eating and nutrition should be given high priority in the school curriculum, at all ages. This should include everyday basic cooking skills, nutritional knowledge and skills to make healthy food choices. Opportunities to achieve this exist in many subject areas.

11 Teaching should focus on the food that children eat as well as on nutritional content if the concepts of healthy eating are to be under-stood and applied.

Promoting a healthy eating pattern needs to start at primary and pre-school age, and then be built on and reinforced throughout school years, to enable children to create or choose foods which form part of a healthy eating pattern. Action at an early age is an investment in children's long-term health.

Nutrition education needs to be expressed in terms of foods as well as nutrients, and will need practical facilities in schools. Teachers also need to encourage critical appraisal of messages in food advertising and promotional information.

SCHOOL MEALS

12 The Department for Education should issue national nutritional guidelines for school catering, such as those produced by The Caroline Walker Trust* as part of the School Meals Campaign, and guidance on their implementation. It should also allocate and ring fence adequate financial resources to maintain an affordable school meals service for all school children.

13 All school catering contracts, whichever organisation holds them (LEA, education board or school governors), should specify nutritional guidelines, and provision should be monitored.

The school meals service can be a valuable source of nutritious food and learn-ing about healthy eating for children. It must be properly resourced, meet nutritional guidelines, be dependable and available to all children. School meals can make a major contribution to healthy eating patterns, and can represent the best nutritional option, and value for money at lunchtime. The Department for

Education, by supporting school meals, will be giving schools a clear lead in promoting healthy eating patterns in school children.

The Caroline Walker Trust guidelines are based on the latest government dietary recommendations, and have been welcomed by government.

GOVERNORS AND PARENTS

14   School governors and school boards should be encouraged to use their influence to introduce and ensure implementation of healthy food policies in schools. Such bodies should be involved in monitoring food services at their school, and require regular reports.

15   Training and information packages developed for school governors and school boards by local and national agencies could support them in this role.

Policy makers in schools need to be made aware of the problems of children's diets, and be involved in the solution. Governors may be able to exert greater influence over the food services provided in their school as contracts are renewed. Training bodies should use the information in this report in training school governors on the importance of, and influences on, child nutrition. The Department for Education should ensure that all governing bodies, and the Scottish Office ensure that all school boards, have a copy of the Caroline Walker Trust's *Nutritional guidelines for school meals.**

Healthy eating policies can improve the nutritional content of the foods consumed by children at school. The implementation of such policies is more effective if done in conjunction with the pupils it will affect. Organisation of the school day must allow sufficient time for children to make considered, guided decisions about their lunchtime food choices.

Schools are under considerable pressure to use classroom materials, posters and vending machines from food manufacturers. These resources often reflect a commercial interest and may undermine healthy eating messages. Parents and governors should be aware of the effects of food messages in food advertising, packaging and promotion.

Monitoring and research

MONITORING

16   Children's progress towards the nutrition targets should be monitored as part of the national strategies for health. The Department of Health should set up a forum to: ensure monitoring of the effect of legislation on children's dietary habits; assess the

nutrition and health implications for children of the policies of other government departments; and recommend action on the results. The recommendations should be discussed and acted on by the appropriate government departments, and the Ministerial Cabinet Committee in England.

17 **Intervention programmes to promote healthy eating must be evaluated to demonstrate their effect on children's knowledge and/or behaviour.**

Changes in legislation will affect children's eating patterns, but there is no systematic collection of data to indicate whether these changes are positive or negative. Existing research and surveys on children's diets, such as the national study of health and growth, could be adapted to monitor impact.

Evaluation of intervention programmes to demonstrate their effect on children's food knowledge and behaviour will improve their adoption in other locations.

RESEARCH

18 **Further research should be undertaken by the Department for Education and others to add to the data on the nutritional quality of children's diets and current food consumption patterns. These data should be examined in relation to changes in national legislation which affect children's eating patterns including, for example, the school curriculum and school meal provision, and food advertising, and the effect of these on children's short-term and long-term health.**

There is a lack of research evidence, particularly on current dietary patterns in early childhood. There is also a need for further longitudinal studies on nutrition and health, which track children through their school years and into adulthood.

---

* *Nutritional guidelines for school meals: Report of an Expert Working Group.* Sharp I. 1992. Published by the Caroline Walker Trust, London. Available from: School Meals, PO Box 7, London W3 6XJ. Price £8.50 (including p & p). Cheques/postal orders payable to 'BSS'.

CHAPTER 4

Cause for concern

Nutritional content of children's diets and the health implications

Dr Michael Nelson
Department of Nutrition and Dietetics,
King's College London

SUMMARY
The diets of UK school children are too high in fat, especially saturated fat, and in sugar. They are too low in iron, calcium, dietary fibre, and probably in anti-oxidant vitamins such as vitamin E. Obesity is becoming more prevalent and, where it occurs, should be tackled as early in childhood as possible. Vegetarian and vegan diets are not in themselves harmful but they can pose risks for children who adopt such diets without sufficient nutritional education.

A poor diet clearly creates short-term health problems in relation to growth, and long-term problems in relation to anaemia, low bone mass, hypertension, coronary heart disease and some cancers. Poorer children may be more vulnerable. A very poor diet is likely to affect children's activity levels and academic performance.

Very little research data is available on children's and young people's eating patterns. The major studies carried out in the 1980s and 1990s are listed in Table 1 on page 19. Only four of the ten studies listed covered a sample greater than 1,000.

TABLE 1: Dietary surveys of school children in the UK, 1979-93

Author	Year	Age	Number	Method
Hackett[1]	1979-81	11-14	405	5 x 3-day diaries
Bull[2]	1982	15-25	913	14-day diary
DHSS[3]	1983	10-11, 14-15	3,296	7-day weighed
Crawley[4]	1986-87	16-17	4,760	4-day diary
Whincup[5]	1987-88	5-7	3,000	24-hour recall
Nelson[6]	1988	7-10, 11-12	227	7-day weighed
McNeill[7]	1988	12	61	7-day weighed
Whincup[8]	1990	5-7	3,000	Food frequency questionnaire
Adamson[9]	1990	11-12	379	2 x 3-day diaries
Nelson[10]	1993	6-10	60	7-day weighed

In 1991 the government published revised quantified nutritional guidelines in the form of Dietary Reference Values, covering 34 nutrients. All the studies in Table 1 show similar patterns of intake: energy, calcium, iron and fibre intakes often below the reference values, and percentage energy from fat and sugar above the reference values.

The Reference Nutrient Intake (RNI) represents the amount of nutrient sufficient for almost all individuals in a group. If the average intake of a group is at the RNI then the risk of deficiency in the group is very small. Energy is expressed as an Estimated Average Requirement (EAR): that is the average requirement of a group for energy. About half the group will usually need more than the EAR and half will need less. RNIs and the EAR for energy vary between boys and girls and between age groups. Figures 1-6 on pages 21-24 show the intakes of children expressed as a percentage of the RNI (or EAR in the case of energy).

Energy intakes

Energy intakes are an indicator of whether children are growing adequately and whether or not they are becoming overweight or obese. In general, the levels of energy intake are adequate for the majority of children in the UK. For some age and sex groups of UK school children the energy intake is slightly over 100% of the EAR, while in other groups it is slightly below.

There is evidence that Body Mass Index (BMI) for boys and for girls aged 11 and 12 has increased between 1980 and 1990, and this has been accompanied by small but significant increments in both height and weight.[9] At least 10% of children could be regarded as overweight.

An important question is whether children with a high BMI are more likely to have a high BMI in adolescence and adulthood. The Bogalusa Heart Study[11] has shown that obesity in childhood is associated with raised blood pressure and raised cholesterol levels and that to some extent these track from childhood into adulthood. There is also evidence that at least 50% of children who are more than 120% of standard weight for age at age 11 will be overweight or obese in early adulthood.

Data from the National Study of Health and Growth[12] show that BMI generally tends to increase from the age of four. The earlier this increase starts, the more likely it is that the child is going to be overweight or obese in adolescence and in adulthood. Therefore to influence the levels of obesity in later life the problem must be tackled in the early primary school years.

When considering energy intakes in children, it is also important to consider children's activity levels. For cardiac health it is recommended that children should be able to sustain a heart rate of over 140 beats per minute (over 120 beats per minute for adults) for periods of up to 20 minutes. In a study of 11-16 year olds, 4% of boys and less than 1% of girls were sustaining these levels of activity.[13]

Fat

The current recommendation is that a maximum of between 33% and 35% of total energy intake* should be derived from fat. However, Figure 1 shows that in every age group of children, energy from fat in the diet exceeds the recommended level, with one exception among eight-year-old girls.

Among adults there is an association between total energy from fat, particularly saturated fat, and the risk of coronary heart disease. There is evidence that the fatty streaks and development of atheroma start in childhood, and particular dietary patterns which are established in childhood may be sustained in adulthood.

Sugar

The current recommendation is that maximum non-milk extrinsic (NME) sugar intake should be between 10% and 11% of total energy*. In all age groups of UK school children the intake of total sugar (intrinsic milk sugars and non-milk extrinsic sugars) is in the region of 20%-23% of total energy. The main health implication of raised NME sugar intake is an increased risk of dental caries. There is no good evidence of a nutrient dilution or 'empty calories' effect: children with

* Range taken from Dietary Reference Values for fat and NME sugars as a percentage of total energy intake and as a percentage of total food energy intake (total energy without alcohol).

FIGURE 1: Percentage energy from fat: Dietary levels in UK school children

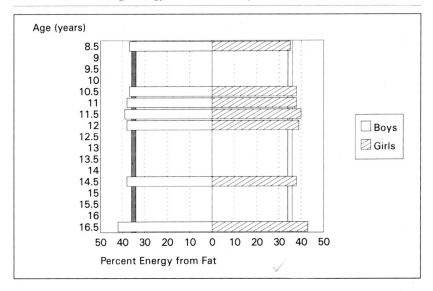

FIGURE 2: Percentage energy from total sugars: Dietary levels in UK school children

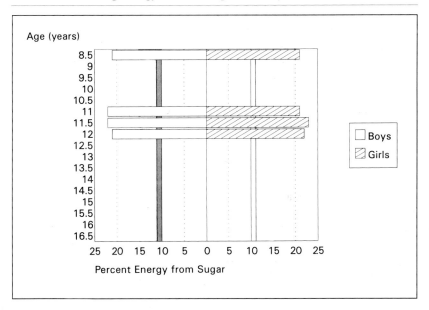

a high percentage of energy from sugar tend to have lower percentage energy from fat, and vice versa, but intake of other nutrients seems to be largely unaffected.[14]

Vitamins C and E

The level of vitamin C intake exceeds the Reference Nutrient Intake (RNI) in almost all age and sex groups (see Figure 3). However, levels of vitamin E are very low in relation to the RNI. Not enough is known yet about the relationship between anti-oxidant vitamin intake and the risks of coronary heart disease and cancer. However, it would seem wise to err on the side of caution and increase the total amount of anti-oxidant vitamins in children's diets.

Claims have recently been made that children who are given vitamin/mineral supplements performed better in non-verbal intelligence tests than children who were given a placebo. However, when the experiment was repeated, no differences were found between the two groups.[6]

FIGURE 3: Vitamin C: Dietary levels in UK school children

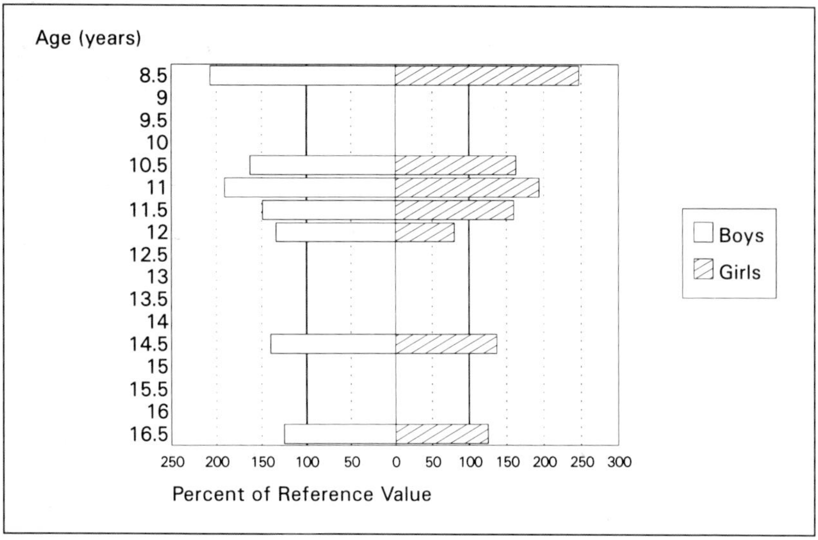

Age (years)

Percent of Reference Value

Boys
Girls

Iron

Levels of iron intake appear to be adequate in primary school children. However, iron intake levels are very low among adolescent children, particularly girls (see Figure 4).

FIGURE 4: Iron: Dietary adequacy in UK school children

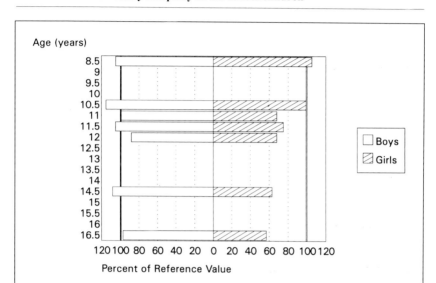

Although these low intakes of iron rarely produce any clinical symptoms, they may be related to reduced immune response, reduced academic and physical performance, and problems relating to long-term health. Children who have a median vitamin C intake and a *low* iron intake are six times more likely to be anaemic compared to children with median vitamin C intake and a *high* iron intake. If anaemia in adolescence tracks into early adulthood, anaemic girls are more likely to give birth to infants of low birthweight, which may be associated with high systolic blood pressures in middle age.

Calcium

Calcium levels appear to be adequate in primary school children, but fall below recommended levels in adolescence, particularly among 11-15 year olds (see Figure 5). Studies suggest that children who drink milk regularly either in childhood or adolescence are more likely to have a higher bone mass than those who only drink milk sometimes or rarely during childhood or adolescence.[15] Osteoporosis is associated with low intakes of calcium and low levels of activity in childhood.

FIGURE 5: Calcium: Dietary adequacy in UK school children

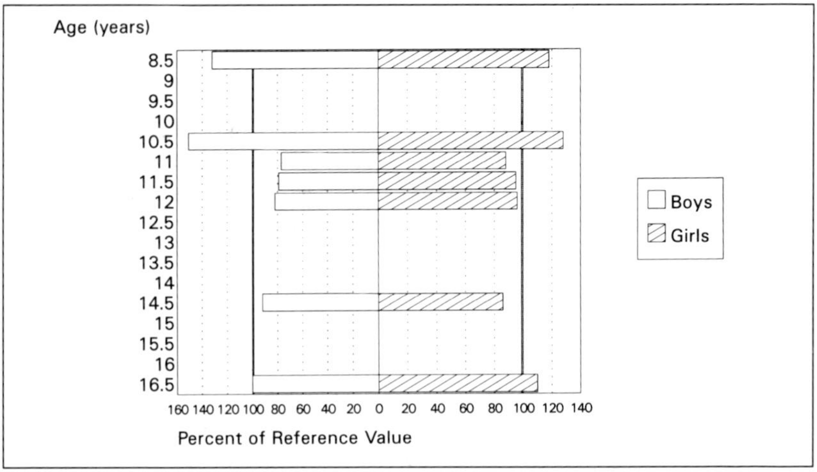

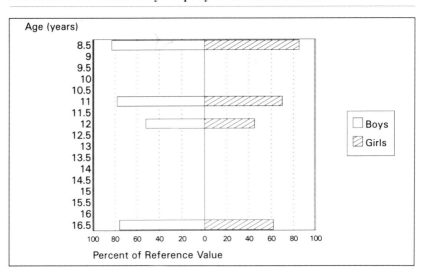

Folic acid

Children in all age and sex groups appear to have folic acid intakes lower than the recommended levels (see Figure 6). In addition to its role in the prevention of anaemia, there is good evidence that high intakes of folic acid can reduce the recurrence of neural tube defects (spina bifida and anencephaly) in affected

FIGURE 6: Folic acid: Dietary adequacy in UK school children

families. If low folic acid intakes persist from childhood into adulthood, this may have adverse effects on the outcome of pregnancy.

Dietary fibre

Current dietary fibre intakes appear to be too low among UK school children in all age and sex groups. Longitudinal studies need to be carried out to find out more about the effects a low fibre intake in childhood may have on subsequent disease in adulthood, particularly risks of large bowel cancer and diverticulosis.

Vegetarian diets

There is some concern that the diets of vegetarian or vegan children may be inadequate. One study reported in 1988 that vegan children have lower energy, fat and calcium intakes, and diets richer in fibre, iron and anti-oxidant vitamins than non-vegan children.[16] Studies of vegetarians show similar results. The growth of children who are vegetarian and vegan seems to be adequate in relation to their energy needs. Children who diet or adopt vegetarian habits without proper guidance increase their risk of poor nutritional status including low protein intake. It is important that children changing to such a diet should be taught how to make an appropriate choice of foods.

Conclusion

Children's diets are below the recommended levels for many nutrients including iron, calcium and anti-oxidant vitamins, and above the recommended levels for fat, saturated fat and sugar. Obesity is becoming more prevalent. In all social class groups children are taller than their counterparts in previous years, but this may be related to improved health in childhood and reduced energy requirements due to decreasing activity levels. However, it is important to remember that many cheap high-calorie foods are high in fat and sugar. Poorer children may also be vulnerable in their micro-nutrient intake, as a varied diet high in micro-nutrients tends to be more expensive. This is an area where school meals could make a major contribution, as they could provide children with foods which they would not normally have at home. Changes made now to children's diets are likely to have both short and long-term benefits.

References

1   Hackett A, Rugg-Gunn AJ, Appleton DR, Eastre JE, Jenkins GN. 1984. A two-year longitudinal nutritional survey of 405 Northumberland children initially aged 11.5 years. *British Journal of Nutrition*; 51: 67-75.

2   Bull N. 1985. Dietary habits of 15 to 25-year-olds. In: *Human Nutrition: Applied Nutrition;* vol 39A: supplement 1: 1- 68.

3   Department of Health and Social Security. 1989. *The diets of British schoolchildren. Subcommittee on Nutritional Surveillance. Committee on Medical Aspects of Food Policy.* Report on health and social subjects 36. London: HMSO.

4   Crawley H. 1991. *The vitamin and mineral intakes of teenagers aged 16/17 years in Britain.* Paper prepared for Booker Nutritional Products.

5   Personal communication, 1993.

6   Nelson M, Naismith DJ, Burley V, Gatenby S, Geddes N. 1990. Nutrient intakes, vitamin supplementation and intelligence in British schoolchildren. *British Journal of Nutrition;* 64: 13-22.

7   McNeill G, Davidson L, Morrison DC, Crombie IK, Keighran J, Todman J. 1991. Nutrient intake in schoolchildren: some practical considerations. *Proceedings of the Nutrition Society*; 50: 37-43.

8   Personal communication, 1993.

9   Adamson A, Rugg-Gunn AJ, Butler T, Appleton DR, Hackett A. 1992. Nutritional intake, height and weight of 11 to 12-year-old Northumbrian children in 1990 compared with information obtained in 1980. *British Journal of Nutrition*; 68: 543-563.

10   Nelson M. 1993. Work in progress.

11   Berenson GS, Srinivasan SR, Webber LS et al. 1991. *Cardiovascular risk in early life: the Bogalusa Heart Study.* Michigan: The Upjohn Company.

12   Chinn S, Rona RJ, Gulliford MC, Hammond J. 1992. Weight-for-height in children aged 4-12 years. *European Journal of Clinical Nutrition;* vol 46: no 7.

13   Armstrong N et al. 1990. Patterns of physical activity among 11-16 year old British children. *British Medical Journal*; 301: 203-5.

14   Naismith DJ, Nelson M, Burley V, Gatenby S. *Does a high sugar diet promote overweight in children and lead to nutrient deficiencies?* Unpublished.

15   Sandler R, Slemenda CW, Laporte RE, Cauley JA, Schramm MM, Baresi ML, Kriska AM. 1985. Post-menopausal bone density, and milk consumption in childhood and adolescence. *American Journal of Clinical Nutrition*; 42: 270-274.

16   Sanders TAB. 1988. Growth and development of British vegan children. *American Journal of Clinical Nutrition*; 48: 822-825.

Children's eating patterns and habits

Ms Anne Lynd-Evans
Local Authority Caterers Association

SUMMARY
Children's eating patterns are affected by many factors. One in nine children go to school without breakfast, and one in six go home to no cooked evening meal. Snacks now form a significant part of children's diets.

School meals can make an important contribution. The challenge to school caterers is to make the 'healthy' choices the 'favourite' choices, so that popular meals are also those which meet nutritional guidelines. Factors influencing children's choice of meal include: money available, mathematical skills, peer pressure, children's familiarity with the range of dishes on offer, and social skills.

Children should be given more basic food education in schools, to help them acquire the basic skills required to choose and eat a healthy diet.

When and what do teenagers eat?

Starting the day without breakfast is normal for one in nine children,[1] and even more common among teenage girls.[2] Many children are therefore extremely hungry by mid-morning, having eaten nothing since the previous evening. Nearly all schools (nine out of ten) sell crisps, sweets, drinks and snacks, and over one-third (34%) of children have a mid-morning snack every day.[3]

Lunch is eaten by nearly all pupils. The proportion of children eating school meals varies from region to region and school to school. A 1992 survey of 200 school children aged 12-17 showed that 45% of children took a school lunch; 26% took a packed lunch; 22% purchased their lunch out of school; and 7% took their lunch at home.[3]

Although the nutritional quality of lunches varies, the school meal often represents the best option, particularly in terms of vitamins and minerals.[4] The cash cafeteria system – which is becoming increasingly common in secondary schools – offers children a wide selection of foods from which to choose. Cash cafeterias have increased the variety of meals consumed. Some children choose a combination of foods which produces a nutritionally balanced meal, but many do not. Some primary schools are also introducing cash cafeterias. Very young children may be confused by having a wider choice of foods, but the system can work well provided that children have enough time to make their choice, and some guidance over their choice, and as long as parents, teachers and governors encourage sensible combinations.

Surveys show that one in six children go home from school to no cooked meal, and half or more consume crisps, snacks and biscuits in place of an evening meal.[1]

Teenagers have considerable spending power: 86% of them receive pocket money. In an average week, 12-year-olds get £2.90 and 16-year-olds get £6.20.[3] Much of this pocket money is spent at confectioners, tobacconists and newsagents, where children and teenagers account for nearly half (49%) of sales.[3] Food and drink items are purchased at these shops by seven out of ten teenagers.[3]

Does health form part of decision-making?

There is a discrepancy between school children's attitudes and their behaviour in terms of whether health forms part of decision-making. A survey of teenage girls carried out by the National Dairy Council in 1989 showed that 80% 'tried to eat healthily most of the time'.[2] However, when children in another survey were asked about the reasons for their choice of school meals, 60% said they made the choice because it was their 'favourite'; 20% because of 'the way it looks'; and only 10% because it was 'healthy'.[1]

Obstacles and opportunities in school catering

The challenge to school caterers is to merge 'favourite' with 'healthy' so that popular meals are also those which meet nutritional guidelines. Simply providing 'healthy choices' which are available in most dining rooms, or in tuckshops, has proved insufficient for the following reasons:
• *Cost.* Some of the 'healthy choices' may be more expensive and thus less attractive to the children.
• *Mathematical ability.* When combining foods to make a meal, pupils will choose a selection they know will be within their spending power. Lack of arithmetic skills makes changing to an unfamiliar selection very risky.
• *Peer pressure.* If a child's friends are all eating one style of food, making a different selection requires a strong personality. If the current trend in the group is to buy burgers and chips, children will follow the trend rather than risk ridicule by choosing a baked potato with baked beans.

• *Speed.* With school catering, children have to make their choices very quickly. Two hundred children are served in 30-40 minutes, leaving only 10 seconds separating each child. Queuing provides an opportunity for displaying information, but there is very little time available to encourage, discuss or consider alternative choices of food.

• *Unfamiliar food.* Many children are reluctant to try new tastes and textures. Hence the need for marketing and promotional techniques to accompany changes. But schools offer an environment where experimentation and learning should be encouraged. It is therefore important to link foods available at school with classroom-based learning.

The way forward

The sensible way forward must be to teach children about the nutritional differences between foods and about the impact that foods can have on their health, and then to help them to put this new knowledge into practice at school.

The ethos of the school, based on a consistent pro-health message in the school policy and reiterated by governors, headteacher and teachers and parents, can have an enormous impact on children's food choice. This ethos must be nurtured if healthy eating is to become a normal part of school life.

References

1   Gardner Merchant. 1991. *School meals survey – 'What today's children are eating'*. London: Burson Marsteller.

2   National Dairy Council. 1989. *Teenage eating habits and attitudes to food.* London: National Dairy Council.

3   Leatherhead Food Research Association. 1992. *Consumer focus no 10. Teenagers – an in-depth study of consumer attitudes and behaviour.* Leatherhead: Leatherhead Food Research Association.

4   Sharp I. 1992. *Nutritional guidelines for school meals: Report of an Expert Working Group.* London: The Caroline Walker Trust.

CHAPTER 5

National and school policy

What changes in national policy could improve children's eating patterns?

Ms Suzi Leather
National Consumer Council

SUMMARY
Individual health and well-being cannot be separated from the trends in the economy as a whole. Poverty has grown rapidly in the 1980s, particularly affecting families with young children. In 1979 one child in ten lived in poverty; by the early 90s, this had risen to over one in four.[1] In trying to improve the nation's diet, the personal circumstances in which people make their food and lifestyle choices must be considered. Economic trends and government policies have caused a deterioration in the diet of low-income families: low-income families eat considerably less of the foods generally recommended as part of a healthy diet than high-income groups. The gap between socioeconomic groups is getting wider. Poverty structures food choice in an unhealthy way. Giving more information on healthy eating to families living at or below income support levels serves only to demoralise and to increase guilt and frustration. Improvement depends rather on a successful anti-poverty strategy. A properly resourced, nutritionally adequate and dependable school meals service is a vital part of such a strategy.

National policy-making in the 80s and early 90s has been based on the belief that individuals are rational actors, able to choose and enact rational choices. The government has provided information and advice about healthy eating, but the responsibility for diet is placed firmly with the individual. The state's responsibility for children's eating patterns has been scaled down considerably, and it has been assumed that families will be able to sustain their new responsibilities.

The emphasis has been on information as the key to behavioural change. Free-market thinking assumes that choices are unconstrained by the factors which really govern people's lives: such as availability of healthy food or access to such food at affordable prices. The government's response to evidence of bad dietary habits is to provide yet more information. This is illustrated in *The health of the nation* strategy for England which states: "Action to achieve health and nutrition targets involves the dissemination of information about healthy eating and encouraging and enabling changes in the population's diet."[2]

But enabling change in very many children's diets is not about more or better targeted information: it is about money. The growth and extent of poverty in the UK is the strongest factor militating against these children's access to a healthy diet.

The growth of poverty

There is overwhelming evidence that disease and ill health visit the poor more often, for longer, more intensely and for a far greater part of their usually shorter lives than the better-off.[3] Recession has intensified many of the factors precipitating illness, by reducing personal incomes and increasing poor housing and stress. Economic policies have led to a marked increase in income inequality, with the poorest becoming worse off not only relatively but absolutely. The population as a whole became 30% better off in the period 1979 to 1988/89, with the income of the richest one-tenth of the population rising by 46% yet the income of the poorest one-tenth falling by 6%. Trends in diet indicate that food poverty is now more widespread, dietary inequalities are more marked and the factors associated with diet-related disease are intensified.

Families with children have been particularly affected by the increase in income inequalities and are now more at risk of living in poverty than in 1979. Families with children account for a greater percentage of the poorest one-tenth of the population now than they did in 1979. The percentage of children living in families dependent on benefits has more than doubled.[4] Factors contributing to the increase in child poverty and deprivation in the 1980s include: economic trends and taxation policy, demographic changes, and changes in social policies.

Economic trends and taxation policy
Unemployment has forced many families into dependence on state benefits.[5] Changes in taxation policy have put families with children behind in relation to single people and childless couples, and the poorest children have come off worst.

The overall tax burden of poor earners with two children has increased from 2.4% to 6.3%, while the tax burden of a family on five times the average male earnings has fallen from 48.8% to 34.5%.[6]

Demographic changes
In 1991, 2.2 million children lived with a lone parent, compared with 1.5 million in 1981.[7] It has been estimated that one-third of all children will experience living in a lone-parent family.[8] The incidence of poverty is much greater in single parent families.[9]

Changes in social policies
Benefits are now tied to prices rather than to earnings. As earnings have moved ahead of prices, the living standard of those on benefit has declined. The value of all major benefits in the UK has dramatically declined in relation to earnings over the last decade. UK spending on social protection as a proportion of GDP did not increase in the 1980s. In fact the proportion of GDP spent on benefits fell by one-fifth in the second half of the decade. The purchasing power of British benefits relative to living costs is now more than 10% below the European Community average.[5]

Child benefit is a universal benefit which is particularly important for low-income families. Yet as it counts as income for the purpose of assessing means-tested income support, its value is deducted from the benefit of the poorest families. The level of child benefit was frozen for three years from 1988-90. Its value for all children except the first is still more than £2 short of its real 1987 level.[10]

Changes in school meals
The 1980 Education Act abolished the national fixed price of the school meal (35p a day in 1979), abandoned minimum nutritional standards, and removed the statutory duty on LEAs to provide school meals for all. The proportion of children taking school meals in England fell from 64% in 1979 to 42% in 1991.[11]

Of the children taking school meals in England, the proportion entitled to free meals grew steadily through the 1980s, peaking at 21% in 1987.[12] In 1988, following further changes in social security legislation, the number of children entitled to free school meals was cut by one-third, and some 400,000 children lost out.[12] The erosion of entitlement continues. In April 1992, the children of 35,000 poor families had their right to free school meals removed.[13] Children of families living on income support still receive a free meal: those on family credit or on low incomes above family credit thresholds do not. Despite the cuts in entitlement, the proportion of children entitled to free school meals is rising, reflecting the increasing number of families on income support.

In 1990, 44% of school aged children had school meals. Just over a quarter of these children had their meals free.[14] On average, take-up of free meals is 75%

of entitlement: higher in primary and lower in secondary schools. The local authority receives an allowance from the Department for Education in respect of how many meals it has to provide for children from families in receipt of income support. Local authorities receive no subsidy for paid school meals (apart from certain European subsidies: see page 35). The meal system must be profitable, and recent legislation requires local authorities to put the school meals service out to private tender. This is known as compulsory competitive tendering. There is no definition of what a meal means, and several LEAs now serve only packed lunches to the children who are entitled to free meals. This means that some children do not have a daily hot meal.

Other pressures on the family budget
Other pressures on the family budget, such as increasing rents and heating costs, have had a significant impact on the money left available for food. Research shows that food expenditure, which is often the only flexible item in the household budget, is squeezed when times are hard. In these circumstances, people buy cheaper, less healthy foods: cheap fatty meats rather than lean meat, white bread rather than wholemeal. They also buy less fresh fruit and vegetables, and some stop buying fresh fruit altogether.

The increase in the rates of rent arrears, mortgage interest payments arrears, and repossessions has led to greater homelessness and increased numbers living in bed and breakfast accommodation. The number of households accepted as homeless by local authorities rose from 63,013 in 1978 to 177,283 in 1991. This represents over a quarter of a million children.

Materials and facilities
People need a cooker, fridge, cooking utensils, storage facilities and a table to eat from. A survey of low-income mothers revealed that only half had a table to eat from.[15] The introduction of the Social Fund means that people are unable to get grants for essential items like this, and almost half of those applying will not succeed in obtaining a loan. Research shows that of those who are successful in getting a loan, over one-third have to cut back on food, clothing or paying bills in order to repay the loan.[16]

The inadequacy of benefit levels
Benefit levels are inadequate. An independent survey of low-income families found that in 1991, 20% of parents and 10% of children in the sample had gone without food in the previous month because of lack of money, no parent or child in the survey was eating a healthy diet, and many parents and children were eating very poor diets.[17]

A couple with two children under 11 receive benefit of £108.75 a week (£5,655 a year), and a couple with three children receive £123.80 a week (£6,437 a year). A single parent with two children aged four and six will have £88.65 a week

(£4,609 a year). Those who have deductions taken from their benefits have much less than this to live on, as do many people who are on very low wages.

Some two million children live in families that are dependent on income support.[1] In 1993, parents had £2.83 a day to meet all the needs of a child under 11, and £3.85 for a child over 11. (These figures are calculated by taking the weekly children's personal allowances plus family premium and dividing by seven.) Research published in 1992 by the Joseph Rowntree Trust showed that income support rates do not permit households with children to reach even a low standard of living, even if the parents do not smoke or drink. The income support rate for a couple with two children under 11 was £36 a week short, and for a lone parent with two children it was £25 a week short.[18] A similar study which pared down the living standard to that which only just enables the maintenance of physical efficiency was carried out. It excluded not only alcohol and tobacco but also water rates, community charges, insurance, social occasions, presents, sweets, trips out and holidays. The cost of this lifestyle for a couple with three children was £128.86 a week, yet the income support rate for such a family was £126.86 a week.

The impact of poverty on diet

Low-income groups eat considerably less of the foods generally recommended as part of a healthy diet than high-income groups: skimmed milk, fish, vegetable oils, fresh fruit and vegetables, wholemeal bread, lean meats, rice and pasta. They eat far more of the foods that people are advised to eat less of: whole milk, eggs, lard, sugar, preserves and white bread. The government argues that low-income families can afford to eat healthily. A diet suggested by the Ministry of Agriculture, Fisheries and Food in 1992 and costing £10 per person per week, would take up over 40% of the income of families living on benefit.[19] Yet many women estimate that, after paying all their bills and debts, they have only £5 per person per week left for food.[20]

The pressure on poor families' budgets has led to a reduction in their consumption of milk, fish, meat, eggs, bread, fruit and vegetables. Their consumption of fresh green vegetables has nearly halved. In larger poor families, the changes are even more marked: consumption of meat and fruit has halved, and consumption of fresh green vegetables has fallen to one-third of its 1980 level.[21] Even this may be overly optimistic for two reasons: firstly because the data are based on a survey which excludes many of the most vulnerable groups such as bedsit families, and secondly because of the bias caused by the tendency for respondents to buy more than usual during the period of the survey.

The trends in income in the 1980s are paralleled by the trends in diet. The gap between socioeconomic groups is getting wider, and many at the bottom are worse off not only relatively but absolutely. At the beginning of the 80s, the poorest families with two children spent on food about 80% of the equivalent spending of a similar family at the top end. By 1991 this percentage had dropped to 66%. Often it is the foods which have health-protective effects that show the greatest consumption inequalities. For example, although fruit consumption for the population as a whole has risen, some low-income families eat less fresh fruit now than they did in the 1950s.[21]

Poverty structures food choice in an unhealthy way. For reasons to do with siting of areas of cheap housing and cost of public transport, poor people are more likely to buy food at small local shops, which usually stock little healthy food and are often as much as 20% more expensive than shops in wealthier areas.[22] Many healthier food options are also more expensive in terms of calories per pence, and may require more fuel in cooking. Finally, it is important to remember that asking people to alter their diet implies experimentation, which involves risk and extra expense. If you do not like the food, you may waste it. How rational, therefore, is it for people on a low income to take these risks?

European policies

The Common Agricultural Policy (CAP) has an enormous impact on the price and availability of over 90% of food, yet it hits the poor harder than the rich. The CAP currently costs the average British family of four between £17 and £18 a week in taxes and higher food prices. The current mechanism for translating European farm prices into sterling always raises our food prices. Since September 1992 when sterling was devalued, food prices overall rose by about 3%, more than cancelling the cuts in support prices negotiated under CAP reform.

The fine tuning of the CAP also has considerable bearing on the availability of healthier foods. In the European Community* in 1990, while poor families struggled to afford fruit, 320,000 tonnes of apples, 120,000 tonnes of tomatoes, 24,500 tonnes of cauliflowers, and 600,000 tonnes of peaches and nectarines were either destroyed or made unfit for human consumption simply in order to keep prices artificially high.[23] The EU currently has a scheme for subsidising milk and milk products to catering companies and local education authorities. The subsidy applies to whole and semi-skimmed milk and yogurts made from this milk. But the subsidy is larger for whole milk than it is for semi-skimmed milk.[24] Such food schemes are merely a means to dispose of some of the surpluses of the less healthy foods on the market. They may therefore be regarded as a hindrance to changing dietary patterns for the better. The European Union has an agriculture policy but no nutrition policy. It needs to have an agriculture policy which is subordinated to the requirements of a nutrition policy.

* Now the European Union

1clusion

There is an urgent need for a holistic approach to healthy eating for children. It should encompass cost and availability of healthy food and an income adequate to cover all living expenses. The family can no longer be relied on to ensure the nutritional health of the nation's children unless there is a massive injection of funds through increased benefit levels and higher wage levels. Yet the trend is to reduce rather than increase benefits, and to depress wages.

The strategy for improving children's diets has to be worked out at a time when many children can only look forward to a further deterioration in their families' already dire financial situation. It is impossible to improve children's diets unless the underlying problem of poverty and deprivation in the UK is tackled first.

If the aim is to set a kind of nutritional floor to children's diets, or at least to stem the worst excesses in the downslide, then there is a need to look outside the confines of the family. The most realistic strategies involve the state assuming a greater responsibility in ensuring the dietary health of children. An obvious expression of this responsibility must be a properly resourced, nutritionally adequate, dependable school meals service. This would be a vital part of a successful anti-poverty strategy. Yet the school meals service is under threat at precisely the time when children need it most. The avowed policy should be a good quality, attractive, free school meals service, available to all children as a right, as both a universal benefit and an important part of a public health programme.

In the short term there must be:

- school meals available to all children who want to buy them, at a price they can afford
- national nutritional guidelines for school meals which take into account the nutritional needs of all school children and current advice about healthy eating
- an expansion of free school meals provision to at least the level available before the April 1988 changes
- sufficient central government funding for school meals to ensure that LEAs or individual schools can operate a high quality school meals service, and
- anti-poverty policies which are sensitive to children: higher child premiums in income support and higher child benefit.

In order to improve children's eating patterns, some of the tenets of free market ideology must be questioned. *The health of the nation*[2] talks about national mass media health education being targeted on groups at particular risk, and identifies lower socioeconomic groups for dietary education. But information is not always the key to changing diet. On a regular basis, parents in the UK are going hungry to ensure that their children are fed. The continual bombardment of these people with advice they cannot afford to follow serves to remind them of their social exclusion but does little to address their dietary ill health. On a deeper level it demoralises them. 'Ought' implies 'can'. If you keep telling people they ought to do something they cannot do, you sever that connection – a connection which is essential to meaningful moral discourse and a sense of self.

References

1   Bradshaw J. 1991. *Child poverty and deprivation in the UK*. London: National Children's Bureau.
2   Department of Health. 1992. *The health of the nation: a strategy for health in England*. London: HMSO.
3   Townsend P, Davidson N, Whitehead M (eds). 1992. *Inequalities in health: The Black Report and The Health Divide*. London: Penguin.
4   In 1979, 1.6 million children (12.2%) lived in households with below half average income. By 1988 this figure had risen to 3.01 million (25.1%). 1991. *Social Security Committee, Low income statistics: Households below average income tables 1988*. London: HMSO.
5   Cross M. 1992. *Parameters of poverty*. Briefing paper prepared for the Poverty Summit, Edinburgh, December 1992. University of Warwick.
6   Child Poverty Action Group. 1993. *Taxes and benefits: steps to rational reform*. London: Child Poverty Action Group.
7   Office of Population Censuses and Surveys. 1993. *Population trends 71*. London: HMSO.
8   Clarke L. 1989. *Children's changing circumstances: recent trends and future prospects*. University of London Centre for Population Studies.
9   Millar J. 1989. *Poverty and the lone-parent family: the challenge to social policy*. Aldershot: Avebury.
10 Press release from Child Poverty Action Group, 23 February 1993.
11 Figures provided by the Department for Education.
12 House of Commons. *Hansard*, 24.7.86; col 450, and from *CIPFA School meals census 1987, 1988 and 1989*.
13 House of Commons. *Hansard*, 27.11.90; col 366.
14 Figures provided by the Department for Education.
15 James J. 1991. Impact of low income on childhood diet. In *Nutrition, social status and health*, Judy Buttriss (ed). London: National Dairy Council.
16 Findings of the Social Policy Research Unit, York University, quoted in the National Association of Citizens Advice Bureaux press briefing, 22 March 1993.
17 National Children's Home. 1991. *Poverty and nutrition survey*. London: National Children's Home.
18 Bradshaw J (ed). 1992. *Household budgets and living standards. Social Policy Research Findings No 31. November 1992*.
19 Leather S. 1992. Less money, less choice. In *Your food: whose choice?* National Consumer Council (ed). London: HMSO.
20 Author's interviews, unpublished.
21 All figures taken from *Household food consumption and expenditure*, annual reports of the National Food Survey Committee. London: HMSO.
22 Undated. *Fat, fizz and fasting*. Bridges Project/Edinburgh District Council.
23 1991. *The agricultural situation in the community*. European Commission.
24 Aid rates effective from 1 January 1993 – 31 March 1993: whole milk and whole milk yogurt 18.42 pence per pint; semi-skimmed milk and semi-skimmed yogurt 11.62 pence per pint. Figures provided by MAFF.

The health promoting school

Mr Ian Young
Health Education Board for Scotland

SUMMARY
Health promotion in schools is a combination of health education within the curriculum and all the other actions a school takes to protect and improve the health of those within it. A health promoting school actively addresses the hidden curriculum (including for example the school meals service and the tuckshop and vending machines policy), and it tries to link the health and caring services with education through the curriculum.

The introduction of a healthy eating policy in a school in Scotland resulted in pupils choosing healthier snacks during the school day. However, it did not alter children's overall consumption of 'unhealthy foods'. The school needs the support of a health promoting environment, if school healthy eating policies are to be successful and have a lasting impact on children's diets.

What do we mean by health promotion in schools?

Health promotion can be viewed as a combination of health education and all the other actions which a school takes to protect and improve the health of those within it. Schools aim to be caring communities which look after the well-being of the pupils and the staff. However, in the past, health education has often been seen only in terms of 'topics' in the primary school or 'subjects' in the secondary school. As a school develops its health education policy and guidelines, it is important that it reviews its own position on the promotion of health throughout all aspects of school life. Two broad principles underlie this:

1   that the individual pupil will be the main focus of all health promoting activities and that, therefore, planning for the health promoting school will require a close look at the knowledge, attitudes and needs of the pupils;
2   that the pupils themselves are actively involved in the health promoting process.

The features of a health promoting school

There are three main elements of a health promoting school:

1 Specific time is allocated to health education.
Health education has a specific time allocation in the formal curriculum, through social education, topics, subjects and multi-disciplinary courses. In Scotland this tends to be provided through subjects such as biology, physical education, home economics and health education or personal and social education. Good health education occurs in a wide variety of classroom settings. For example, it could include the English teacher discussing self-esteem in a piece of literature.

Home economics is under considerable pressure and does not have a guaranteed place in the curriculum in England, whereas in Scotland it still features in the curriculum for all boys and girls in the first two years of secondary school. Young people attend school for about 15,000 hours between the ages of 5-16, yet in Scotland only approximately 150 hours (1%) are devoted to education about eating or preparing food in the core curriculum. The proportion may be even lower in other parts of the UK.

2 The hidden curriculum is considered.
The health promoting school considers the 'hidden curriculum', which includes the caring relationships developed between home and school and the school's physical environment and facilities. The hidden curriculum includes features such as the school meals service, tuckshops, the provision of vending machines, the relationships between parents and teachers, and the exemplar role of teachers.

3 Links are made with the health and caring services.
The health and caring services play a part in providing health screening and immunisation, as do the psychological and social work services in the support which they provide.

Table 2 illustrates the differences between traditional health education and a health promoting school.

A research study

A study of secondary school pupils carried out in Lothian Region in 1992 investigated the effect of a school's healthy eating health promotion initiative on the knowledge, attitudes and behaviour of pupils.

Pupils in school A, which had introduced a healthy eating policy, were compared with pupils in two control schools (B and C). School A had changed its school tuckshop into a restaurant. It sold no traditional confectionery, ordinary crisps, or high sugar fizzy drinks. Instead it offered wholemeal bread sandwiches, dried fruit and nut mixes, lower fat crisps, yogurt-covered peanuts, and fresh fruit.

TABLE 2: Moving from traditional school health education towards the health promoting school

	Traditional health education	The health promoting school
1	considers health education only in limited classroom terms	takes a wider view including all aspects of the life of the school and its relationship with the community, eg developing the school as a caring community
2	emphasises personal hygiene and physical health to the exclusion of wider aspects of health	is based on a model of health which includes the interaction of physical, mental, social and environmental aspects
3	concentrates on health instructions and acquisition of facts	focuses on active pupil participation with a wide range of methods and on developing pupil skills
4	lacks a coherent, co-ordinated approach which takes account of other influences on pupils	recognises the wide range of influences on pupils' health and attempts to take account of pupils' pre-existing beliefs, values and attitudes
5	tends to respond to a series of perceived problems or crises on a one-off basis	recognises that many underlying skills and processes are common to all health issues and that these should be pre-planned as part of the curriculum
6	takes limited account of psychosocial factors in relation to health behaviour	views the development of a positive self-image and individuals taking increasing control of their lives as central to the promotion of good health
7	recognises the importance of the school and its environment only to a limited extent	recognises the importance of the physical environment of the school in terms of aesthetics and direct physiological effects on pupils and staff
8	does not consider actively the health and well-being of staff in the school	views health promotion in the school as relevant to staff well-being and recognises the exemplar role of staff
9	does not involve parents actively in the development of a health education programme	considers parental support and co-operation as central to the health promoting school
10	views the role of school health services purely in terms of health screening and disease prevention	takes a wider view of the school health services which includes screening and disease prevention but also attempts actively to integrate services within the health education curriculum and helps pupils to become more aware as consumers of health services

Reproduced from *Promoting good health: Proposals for action in schools*, published by the Scottish Health Education Group, 1990.

Drinks on offer included fruit juices and plain and flavoured semi-skimmed milk.

The school handbook given to school A parents included a statement about the NACNE nutrition guidelines and about the school's health education policy. It pointed out that the school was not trying to change everyone's eating habits, but merely to have a healthy influence on young people's choices while they were at school. Meetings were held with parents to explain what the school was doing to promote healthy eating on the school premises.

The study demonstrated that although the levels of knowledge of healthy eating were similar in all three schools, there were statistically significant differences in eating behaviour between the schools. Pupils in school A chose healthier snacks: biscuit and sweet consumption were lower and sandwich consumption was higher than in the control schools.

The uptake of school meals was greater in school A. However, other factors may be involved in this trend, such as the size of catchment areas and the ease with which pupils can return home at lunchtime.

The 150 children in the survey were asked where they got their knowledge about healthy eating from. Not one pupil mentioned friends as a source of information (in contrast to the topic of sexuality where a very high proportion of information comes from friends).

The following two results of the survey illustrate the point that wider factors, outside the domain of the school, may have counteracted school A's achievements, and that health promoting schools need to operate within a health promoting environment.

Firstly, whole milk consumption outside school was higher among pupils in school A than in schools B and C, even though school A supplied only semi-skimmed milk. Statistics from the Scottish Milk Marketing Board indicate that more full fat milk is consumed in rural areas of Scotland than in urban areas. In rural Scotland, more people get their milk from door deliveries of milk than from supermarkets, and semi-skimmed is not always available in door deliveries in rural Scotland. As school A has a wide catchment area including a small town as well as several villages, the high consumption of full fat milk might be the result of parental influence on choice of milk.

Secondly, although school A's healthy eating policy had an impact on children while they were at school, it did not affect children's overall consumption of 'unhealthy foods' over a one-week period (including food and drinks taken both at school and elsewhere).

School A had made a major commitment to promote healthy eating. It is clear that if school healthy eating policies are to be successful and have a lasting impact on children's diets, the school also needs the support of a health promoting environment.

CHAPTER 6

Promotion: help or hindrance?

Marketing food to children

Ms Diane McCrea
Consumers' Association

SUMMARY
The food and drink industry spends millions of pounds promoting their products among children. A large proportion of children's pocket money is spent on sweets, snacks and soft drinks. Children also exert pressure on their parents to buy particular products. The food and drink industry uses various promotion methods to target children, including sponsorship of computer games, character licensing, TV advertising, promotions and special packaging, scout badge sponsorships and the provision of resource materials for schools, and such food promotion affects children's choice of foods. Few of the heavily promoted products encourage a healthy diet. This overall pattern of food promotion may undermine nutritional messages.

Children are big business for the food industry. By the year 2000 there will be almost eight million children aged between 5 and 14 – a 10% increase on 1993 figures. Children under 12 are given an average of £1.40 a week pocket money, much of which they spend on sweets, snacks and drinks. Children also exert an influence on the food their parents buy. In 1990, over 140 new products directly aimed at children were launched in the UK. Over half of these were sugar and chocolate confectionery, soft drinks and snack food.[1]

When food companies market their products to children, they also need to make sure that the products are acceptable to parents. A St Ivel yogurt, launched with the name Fiendish Feet and packaged in a yogurt pot moulded with feet, was withdrawn because parents thought it was too gimmicky, and wanted a better quality yogurt rather than a gimmicky pot. The product was re-launched with simpler packaging, a better quality yogurt and the new name Fiendish Faces.[2]

Marketing people have identified two categories of children. 'Trolley loaders' surreptitiously load the shopping trolley with goods which are not found until after the parent has passed through the checkout. 'Naggers' or 'pesterers' are children who exasperate their parents into buying particular products, usually savoury snacks, sweets, soft drinks and cereals – the products which are heavily advertised.

These heavily promoted foods now make up a large proportion of the average child's diet. In 1980, a study of 11-year-olds found that chips and crisps together were their largest single source of energy intake.[3] A 1990 study revealed that every week, the average British 11-year-old consumed the equivalent of: four packets of crisps, six cans of soft drink, seven bars of chocolate or other sweets, and seven biscuits.[4] In 1992, research by the Consumers' Association[5] revealed that one in four secondary school children ate more than two packets of crisps on an average school day. Nearly half had two or more chocolate bars or sweets each day, and one in four had no fruit or vegetables at all.

How children are targeted (*Tecуniquer*)

1 Computer games
Seventy-three per cent of 5-14 year olds have access to computers, and a growing number of computer games are sponsored by food companies. A pioneer was James Pond 2: Robocod. As the game unfolds, Robocod, a fish-like character, collects Penguin biscuits, some half the size of the screen. Research has shown that 18% of all 5-14 year olds have played the game. Each game is used for an average total of 25 hours.

2 Character licensing
Food companies need to get a licence to use established characters such as Thomas the Tank Engine, Bart Simpson, Batman or Mickey Mouse. In 1991, Disney signed a licensing agreement with Nestlé, giving it the rights to use Mickey Mouse, Goofy and friends on all its food products across Europe for 11 years in a deal worth £70 million.

3 Television advertising
In 1990 advertisers spent over £460 million on advertising their food and soft drinks on TV. A 1990 study by the Food Commission[6] found that if a child watched commercial television for one hour after school each day and all Saturday

morning, he or she would see 92 advertisements for food and drink in one week – nearly 10 an hour. Almost 80% of these advertisements would be for foods which were high in fats, sugars or both. Only 10% of the advertisements could be said to encourage a healthy diet.

4 Promotions and packaging

Clubs. Sainsbury's make their own-brand children's cereal unique by having a breakfast club; joining Burger King Kids Club entitles children to get a 'Super Official Totally Secret Membership Kit'.

Sponsorship. Kia Orange, which is reported to hold 30% of the total soft drinks market, is to sponsor the ASA Swimming Awards for four years.

Promotions. Children's breakfast cereals very often have special offers and free gifts.

Detail and wrapping. Children like food which is specially packaged for them: for example juice cartons with straws, individually wrapped cheese triangles, mini-cake rolls or small yogurts.

5 In the scout hut

Flora is the first company to sponsor the scouts' cook badges. To get these badges, scouts must demonstrate their cooking skills by cooking potatoes in four different ways, plan a menu for one week, and know the importance of a balanced diet. Flora is providing recipe leaflets and soon 36,000 scouts will be wearing the Flora Cook Badge.

6 In the school

Organisations including the Sugar Bureau and the British Egg Information Service have sent teachers free or subsidised resource materials for use in schools. There is also an increasing number of vending machines in schools, selling sweets, chocolates, crisps and canned drinks. The companies that rent out the vending machines dictate what goes into the machines in return for taking responsibility for stocking and maintenance, so schools cannot usually choose to have fruit or other food choices in them. The vending machines generate income for the school on a no-outlay, no-maintenance basis, which cash-strapped schools may find hard to resist.

References

1 Leatherhead Food Research Association. July 1991. *Children's eating habits. An in-depth study of the attitudes and behaviour of children aged 6-11.* Leatherhead Food Research Association.

2 Food frenzy: Marketing food to children. In *Which? Way to Health*: February 1993.

3 Hackett A, Rugg-Gunn AJ, Appleton DR, Eastre JE, Jenkins GN. 1984. A two year longitudinal nutritional survey of 405 Northumberland children initially aged 11.5 years. *British Journal of Nutrition;* 51: 67-75.

4 Adamson A, Rugg-Gunn AJ, Butler T, Appleton DR, Hackett A. 1992. Nutritional intake, height and weight in 11-12 year old Northumbrian children in 1990 compared with information obtained in 1980. *British Journal of Nutrition*; 68: 543-563.

5 Carol Williams and Patricia Ward, Food and Health Research Group. 1993. *School meals. What parents think. What children eat. A detailed report of a national survey of parents' views and the nutritional analysis of one-day food diaries from seven classes of school children, May 1992.* Consumers' Association Limited. (Available from Food and Health Research Group, Association for Consumer Research, 2 Marylebone Road, London NW1 4DF.)

6 The Food Commission. 1990. Sweet persuasion – a diet of junk food ads. *The Food Magazine*; issue 9, vol 1.

CHAPTER 7

Case studies

Five seminars provided an opportunity for conference delegates to discuss some of the issues raised at the conference. Each presented information about an innovative or developing initiative to improve children's eating patterns. Delegates were asked to address four key questions during the discussion:

1 Which professional discipline took the lead in this work? Who else was involved and why? What role did professional organisations play in endorsement or 'ownership'?
2 Does the project add to, or identify any gaps in, research-based knowledge?
3 What evaluation has been done? Is the project sustainable and can it be replicated in other similar settings?
4 What action could be taken to sustain, promote and develop further work in this area?

The case studies and discussions are summarised on the following pages.

TABLE 3: Summary of case studies	Eat your words	School meals assessment project	Health promoting schools in Wales	Multi-disciplinary involvement in promoting school catering	Developing national policy on food advertising to children
Professional discipline which took the lead in the work, and other people involved	A 'healthy alliance' involving experts in health, nutrition and food policy, and education. The alliance spanned national and local organisations.	A national/local alliance. Multi-disciplinary, including experts in health, nutrition, catering and education.	Multi-disciplinary: health and education professionals, parents and governors.	Multi-disciplinary, including health, education and catering professionals.	A 'healthy alliance' took the lead in producing the report.
How the project adds to or identifies gaps in research-based knowledge	Contributes to research-based knowledge by translating national policy issues, such as food labelling and food advertising, into resources for children.	Identified gaps in research in relation to the effects of legislation on school meals and on the cost impact of healthy school catering.	The project has illustrated that children's food purchasing patterns can change.	Identified gaps in collecting information on current school meals consumption patterns among children.	Adds to research-based knowledge by linking food advertising to diet, and by making new policy recommendations.
Evaluation. How the project can be sustained/replicated in other similar settings	Evaluated among teachers, pupils, and health and education experts. The materials will be published and available nationally.	Evaluated among dietitians, health promotion officers, caterers, client officers, teachers and pupils. The materials will be published and available throughout the UK.	The model can be replicated in other similar settings throughout the country.	No evaluation to date.	Expert comment on the report has been incorporated. The report has been published and widely disseminated.
Action which could be taken to sustain, promote and develop further work in this area	* The advertising codes of practice need to be revised so that food advertising supports rather than undermines healthy eating messages. * Funding is needed in order to publish the *Eat your words* materials. * The school curriculum must incorporate teaching on food skills and nutrition.	* Monitoring of nutritional quality must be included in all school catering contracts. * The materials need to be disseminated through professional networks.	* The active involvement of school governors, head teachers and the health authority in discussion with caterers is needed in the development of new school meals contracts, to include nutritional guidelines.	* The responsibility of the director of public health in relation to school meals and children's diets needs to be recognised. * School policies on vending machines and playground vans are needed. * Teaching staff and governors need to recognise the importance of the school meals service.	* Consumer pressure is needed to improve food advertising to children. * There need to be discussions on potential improvements to food advertising with advertisers, regulatory bodies and government.

Eat your words

Ms Imogen Sharp
National Forum for Coronary Heart Disease Prevention

Children receive messages about food and health from many sources. *Eat your words* is a cross-curricular teaching resource which aims to help primary school children to become discerning food consumers by examining the source and content of food information and comparing it with national guidelines for healthy eating. The materials translate national policy issues into worksheets for school children, and encourage children to assess critically the food messages they receive from different sources such as food labelling, advertisements, packaging, shop marketing policies, and health education and promotional materials. The teaching materials are divided into five sections:

1   *What is a healthy diet?* Food groups, personal food choices
2   *What is in our food?* Ingredients, nutritional labelling, health claims, packaging
3   *The persuaders.* Food advertising
4   *Shopping and choice.* Shops, supermarket design and policies
5   *Helpful or unhelpful?* Information sources: commercial and non-commercial.

The worksheets are intended to increase children's awareness of nutrition and product promotion and to encourage discussion in the classroom.

Eat your words has sparked several local and national initiatives, including a school visit to a local supermarket to explore its selling tactics; a video of school activity on the project; and an exhibition of children's work. Several schools also participated in a Scramble-an-Ad competition, in which children were asked to alter or 'scramble' the slogan and pictures of existing food or drink advertisements to reveal their understanding of the hidden messages. Some of the ideas generated in *Eat your words* have also been incorporated in a British Heart Foundation newsletter on nutrition, distributed to all UK secondary schools.

Eat your words has been extensively tested among pupils and teachers, and among experts in health and education. It has been received enthusiastically and several publishers have shown an interest in the materials. The pack is due to be published by the National Forum for Coronary Heart Disease Prevention in 1994.

The *Eat your words* project is a successful example of the type of healthy alliances identified in the national health strategy, promoting active partnerships between the local authority, schools, health services, professional and voluntary organisations and consumer groups.

The resource materials have been produced as a joint venture by the National Forum for Coronary Heart Disease Prevention, the British Dietetic Association, Hampstead, Bloomsbury and Islington Health Promotion Department, and Camden Local Education Authority. The project was initially funded by a Consumers' Association Jubilee Award.

School meals assessment pack

Ms Gill Cawdron
National Forum for Coronary Heart Disease Prevention

The *School meals assessment pack* (SMAP) is a simple, easy-to-use computer program which can calculate the approximate nutritional content of a menu of secondary school meals. The results show a score for energy plus 11 nutrients: fat, saturated fat, starch, non-milk extrinsic sugars, fibre, protein, iron, calcium, vitamin A, folate and vitamin C. The results are produced in the form of bar charts and compare the average meal entered with recommended lunchtime guidelines, indicated by a score of 100 on the bar chart (see Figure 7 below).

FIGURE 7: Example of a menu assessment made by the *School meals assessment pack* computer program

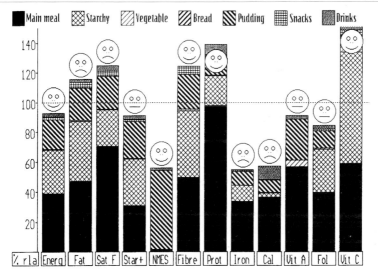

The *School meals assessment pack* can be used by a wide range of people. The pack includes two user guides. The *User's handbook* is for school governors, parents, dietitians, school nurses, health promotion officers, caterers, and client officers (contract monitoring officers), who can use the program as a guide to identify areas of the menu which need improvement. The *Teacher's guide* enables the program to be used in the classroom by 11-16 year old pupils to examine their selection of meals at lunchtime. SMAP has been extensively tested among these groups.

SMAP evolved from a need identified at a conference on *Coronary heart disease prevention in school-age children*, organised in 1988 by the National Forum for Coronary Heart Disease Prevention. Given the range of foods available in secondary schools, and the abolition of nutritional guidelines in 1980, average nutritional content was difficult to assess. A Forum working group developed a resource to fill the gap, drawing on member organisations of the Forum for expertise. *The School meals assessment pack* is a joint initiative between the National Forum for Coronary Heart Disease Prevention, the British Dietetic Association, and Camden and Islington Community Services NHS Trust. It will be published by the Forum in 1994. The project has received funding from the Health Education Authority and the British Heart Foundation.

The prototype computer program was tested in secondary schools in the London Borough of Camden in conjunction with Hampstead Public Health Department. The materials were then piloted nationally, with the involvement and support of organisations such as the British Dietetic Association, the Local Authority Caterers Association, the Health Education Authority and the Health Visitors' Association.

Work on SMAP has helped to spark other initiatives: *Eat your words*, a resource pack to help 9-11 year olds to examine critically food messages (see page 48); the School Meals Campaign, which united 57 national organisations in a call for nutritional guidelines for school meals; development by The Caroline Walker Trust of *Nutritional guidelines for school meals*; and representation of the Forum on the Catering Working Group of the Health of the Nation Nutrition Task Force.

Health promoting schools in Wales

Ms Sue Bowker
Health Promotion Wales

Ms Sue Allerston
Mid Glamorgan Local Education Authority

Promoting healthy eating in a health promoting school

A multi-disciplinary group was set up in Mid Glamorgan:
- to determine the principles of healthy eating in the school environment and to influence schools to implement these principles, and
- to improve the nutritional content of school meals, tuckshops and packed lunches.

The people involved in the group were:

Health and health education professionals: the health promotion manager, district dietetic adviser, chief administrative dental officer, district dental health promotion coordinator and a GP.

Education and school governor representatives: the health education advisory teacher and the development officer from the Governor Support Unit.

Catering: a senior catering inspector and a deputy director of catering services.

Local commerce: the consumer services officer from Tesco.

The group assessed the dietary environment in schools through a questionnaire to headteachers in the pilot area. An individual school was selected for a pilot initiative on school meals, tuckshops and packed lunches. The conference seminar concentrated on the tuckshop initiative.

The pilot school was given support to help reorganise its tuckshop. The children were closely involved in setting up the project, helping to design new tuckshop stalls, staffing the tuckshop, ordering the stock, and counting and banking the proceeds. Items on sale included fresh fruit (delivered to the tuckshop twice a week), plain lower fat crisps, unsweetened popcorn, plain digestive biscuits, breadsticks, nuts, raisins and milk.

The tuckshop led to healthier snacks for the children. Although there was a slight drop in profit, attributable to the smaller range of products on sale, the school is delighted with the substantial profit that it is still able to make while offering healthier snacks to the pupils. It is intended that the pilot project be disseminated to other local schools and eventually to all schools in the county.

The importance of the school dietary environment is stressed in this pilot project. It is, however, equally important to consider the taught curriculum in the health promoting school.

Useful publications

A set of three wallcharts showing links between health education and National Curriculum subjects and religious education has been produced by Health Promotion Wales, working with the Curriculum Council for Wales. These are called: *Opportunities for health education within the National Curriculum* for Key Stages 1 and 2, Key Stage 3 and Key Stage 4, and are supported by booklets for each phase.

Health Promotion Wales has also produced *Cledwyn's Castle,* a pack for preschool playgroups and nurseries. The pack covers a wide range of health issues and includes recipe cards and songs about healthy food, as well as guidelines for parents. It is currently available only in limited quantities.

Work has also begun on a series of handbooks for governors and parents. *Healthy schools for Wales: Governor and parent involvement in health promotion* lists some research findings related to aspects of health and offers suggestions for schools to consider. A handbook on school meals, packed lunches and tuckshops is planned.

Contact addresses

Ms Sue Bowker
Schools Sector Adviser
Health Promotion Wales
Ffynnon-las
Ty Glas Avenue
Llanishen
Cardiff CF4 5DZ

Ms Sue Allerston
Health Education Advisory Teacher
Mid Glamorgan Local Education Authority
Education Resources Centre
Grawen Street
Porth
Mid Glamorgan CF39 OBU

Multi-disciplinary involvement in promoting school catering

Ms Susan Stainton
Essex Food Services, Essex County Council

The county of Essex has about 700 schools. A Health and Food Promotion Group was formed to promote healthy eating in schools. The group involves Essex County Council, the local health authority, advisory teaching groups, and the catering service. The group has been involved in the following three initiatives:

- The 'Teddy Health Promotion Campaign', which is aimed at 1-6 year old children. Four booklets and a *Fun food pack* have been produced for use in playgroups and nursery groups.
- Production of a pack covering school meals and other health and safety topics, which is issued to all new school entrants by the school nurse.
- After-school meetings have been organised for parents to learn more about the school meals service and to sample the meals. However, most parents attending the meetings are well informed about healthy eating issues.

Essex County Council has been involved in the production of various teaching packs, including *Healthy eating: A primary school project.* The success of the project depended on the enthusiasm of individual headteachers and the importance they attach to healthy eating. Motivating decision-makers will be key to the future of school catering and meeting nutritional guidelines.

The schools catering service operates a county-wide controlled primary menu, offering a choice of items which provide young people with the opportunity to make healthier choices. It has also helped schools to set up healthy tuckshops, by locating a supplier who could provide small items of fruit.

Promoting and sustaining healthy eating within a school setting is a long-term activity. By gradually building on existing knowledge, and making small changes in the foods available, the 'eating ethos' of the school can be moved in a positive direction. However, many decisions are being taken on a short-term basis which hinders long-term planning. Continuing, long-term catering contracts, and stability in the organisations which interact as part of the multi-disciplinary team, would enable a sustained programme to promote healthy eating in schools.

Contact address
Ms Susan Stainton, Catering Manager, Essex Food Services, Essex County Council, 3a Montrose Road, Chelmsford, Essex CM2 6TE

Developing a national policy on food advertising to children

Ms Sue Dibb
National Food Alliance

The National Food Alliance Working Party on Advertising is concerned that the nature and extent of food advertising to children undermines public health and nutrition policies. *Children: Advertisers' dream, nutrition nightmare?* is a comprehensive review of the food advertising aimed at children and of the role it plays in influencing food choices. The report considers advertising to children in the context of public health policy and the regulations controlling advertising, and makes recommendations to promote more responsible advertising of food to children.

The foods that are most highly advertised to children as attractive and desirable food choices are the kinds of foods which are unlikely to contribute significantly to a healthy diet. For example, a survey of children's television during one week in May 1992 revealed the following proportions of advertising of food and soft drinks:

Sweetened cereals	32%
Confectionery	16%
Fast food	10%
Bagged snacks	6%
Soft drinks	6%
Butter	6%
Milk	6%
Ice cream	4%
Others	14%

Food Commission, 1992

The National Food Alliance report includes the following options for more responsible food advertising to children:

1   Children's television could be an 'ad-free' or 'restricted ad' zone.

2   There could be a restriction or ban on advertising certain categories of food products to children.

3   Ways in which foods are advertised could be regulated.
a) Foods and soft drinks could always be depicted as being consumed at recognisable mealtimes.
b) The use of characters/personalities could be restricted.
c) Advertising of foods high in fats and/or sugar could be accompanied by health warnings.

4   Frequency of advertising could be limited.

5   Advertising authorities could be obliged to ensure that advertisements for food and soft drinks aimed at children promote a more nutritionally balanced and varied diet.

6   Other funding options could be considered.
a) A levy on particular food advertisers could be made to allow the Health Education Authority to fund generic nutrition messages to children.
b) Subsidised rates of advertising could be offered to advertisers of foods such as fresh fruit and vegetables.

The advertising industry response
The advertising industry argues strongly for 'freedom of commercial speech'. The principle that advertising should not encourage dangerous or unhealthy behaviour is well established, but in the area of food advertising to children it is widely flouted, argues the National Food Alliance. Are the advertising regulatory authorities acting responsibly by permitting a situation which in effect runs counter to and undermines official government health policy? The National Food Alliance believes that food advertisers have a responsibility towards public health and that the advertising regulators should translate that responsibility into clear rules for good practice.

Copies of *Children: Advertisers' dream, nutrition nightmare?* are available from the National Food Alliance, price £25 (£7.50 to voluntary and public interest groups).

Contact address
Ms Sue Dibb
National Food Alliance
3rd floor
5-11 Worship Street
London EC2A 2BH

Discussion and key points
from the case studies

A summary of the key issues identified in each project is given in Table 3 on page 47. A number of common themes emerged from the seminars.

Who should be involved in promoting healthy eating among children?

A multi-disciplinary approach is important and key decision-makers need to be involved when establishing policies which will affect children's diets. Simple guidelines on opportunities to promote healthy eating both outside and within the school – covering youth clubs, leisure facilities, school vending machines, tuck shops selling fruit and vegetables, and school catering – are needed. These issues should be raised in training, including school governor training, within the concept of the health promoting school and environment.

Whose support is needed?

Many organisations have voiced their concern about children's diets and their support for initiatives promoting healthy eating. Three groups emerged as having a potential major impact on the issue:

- medical and health professionals
- decision-makers and those who influence children's food choices, and
- those who provide catering services.

Development and dissemination of resources will need financial support and the support of professional networks.

The food industry, such as the manufacturers and suppliers of foods for vending machines, need to appreciate a consumer demand for 'healthy choices'. This means that public opinion and consumer demand must be harnessed to motivate change. Examples of success include changes to the sugar content of baby foods and the availability of reduced salt and reduced sugar canned products.

Research areas identified

Several areas for research emerged:

- Research on children's food consumption patterns, including fruit and vegetables, and a comparison with other countries. Comparisons with children's exposure to food advertising and marketing in other countries could also be made.
- A study to track the effect that influences on food choice have on diet: for example cost, advertising, marketing and habit. (MAFF has funded research in this area, and is due to report in 1995.)
- User-friendly labelling of the nutritional content of individual foods and their comparative contribution to an overall dietary pattern.
- A long-term demonstration project to illustrate that school catering which

meets nutritional guidelines is not more expensive, when it is a part of a coordinated and well supported schoolwide programme.

- The need to monitor the effects of changes in legislation related to school meals: for example local management of schools.
- Efficacy – the need for the collection of baseline and follow-up data to evaluate interventions to promote healthy eating patterns.

Legislation and codes of practice

The recommendations and actions of the Nutrition Task Force, set up as part of the government's strategy for health in England, will help shape government policy. The issues, projects and recommendations of the conference should be brought to the attention of the Nutrition Task Force.

Legislation or codes of practice which directly contradict or do not promote the dietary targets of *The health of the nation* should be revised. Examples include: the lack of food and nutrition skills in the National Curriculum; European Community subsidies which financially penalise schools and school caterers who switch to lower fat dairy products; and the current advertising regulations which mean that food advertising to children may undermine rather than support the *Health of the nation* targets.

It is important to monitor the effect of changes in legislation. For example, if school catering budgets are further devolved to individual schools, will provision improve or be reduced to the legal minimum? What effect has compulsory competitive tendering had on school meal provision? Has the absence of home economics in the National Curriculum had any effect on children's knowledge and understanding of food choice and preparation skills?

Ideas on the mechanisms for action

Promoting a healthy diet will involve changing policies and provision, to enable children to make food choices which meet nutritional criteria. It does not simply mean giving more information.

There is a need also to recognise and overcome obstacles to changing food provision, such as concern over the financial implications of those changes. Coordinated initiatives with promotion and marketing in a whole-community approach avoids all the responsibility and effort falling on one member of a complex system of influences on children's diets.

Any information must be appropriately communicated throughout the multidisciplinary team, and form part of training programmes.

Long-term planning is necessary to achieve long-term, substantial change, but at present there is a 'short-term' planning climate. Breaking down the large task of change into short-term achievable targets (eg increase in sales of fruit and vegetables within the school) will stimulate change over time.

CHAPTER 8

Discussion

Nutrition and health

Children's diets are high in fat, particularly saturated fat, and sugar, and low in fibre, iron, calcium and some vitamins. Although children are generally taller, they are also fatter than in the past.

This type of diet may contribute to a variety of health problems, in childhood and in later life. The short-term health implications of this type of diet – tooth decay, overweight and anaemia – are evident. The seeds of adult diseases such as coronary heart disease, stroke, some cancers, obesity and low bone mass, are also sown in childhood. Longitudinal tracking studies are needed to consolidate the growing evidence of these long-term health implications.

There are substantial health benefits in a diet that is low in fat and sugar, and high in starchy foods such as bread and cereals, with plenty of fruit and vegetables.

Eating patterns and styles

The nutritional content of children's diets has not improved in the late 1980s and early 90s. Children's eating patterns *have* changed, and for some children snacking or grazing patterns predominate. Many of the snack foods children consume are high in fat and sugar, reflecting the predominance of this type of food in advertising to children.

Children have a vast choice of foods available to them, but their ability to make a healthy choice is constrained by several factors: cost; knowledge; confidence to try new food combinations; and availability of foods which meet cultural, religious or nutritional criteria.

Opportunities within education to learn about nutrition and health need to co-ordinate classroom-based learning with the food children experience at school from vending machines, tuckshops and school meals. The health promoting school also needs a health promoting environment, so that the experience at school is not undermined. The food messages conveyed through advertising and marketing, on television and in shops, for example, could be powerful influences for health.

National policies

A fiscal and agricultural policy that supports a national nutritional policy would prevent some of the contradictory legislation that exists. The most obvious example is to reverse the European dairy product subsidy. Currently the subsidy gives a financial incentive to use high fat dairy produce in preference to low fat varieties in school catering.

Poverty affects one in four children in the UK, and affects the nutritional content of their diet. Fat and sugar are cheap sources of energy. It is insufficient simply to inform; legislation to address poverty is required in order to enable people to act on the information.

One area requiring new legislation is free school meals. Entitlement to free school meals has been reduced and uptake of free meals is limited by under-standing of eligibility and by the social stigma attached to free meals.

The meals that are provided at school may be the only substantial meal of the day. Nutritional guidelines and financial backing for the school catering service are vital to maintain and improve nutritional quality, availability and affordability.

Action for change

Promoting healthy eating among children is a wide-reaching, collective respon-sibility. The key decision-makers will include government, health professionals, educators, caterers, food producers, retailers and consumers. Can health concerns compete with financial concerns? Should they even be in competition? Clear, achievable targets to promote a long-term healthy eating ethos should be made apparent to every decision-maker. School policies on tuckshops, school cater-ing, and vending machines should be developed and put into practice in consultation with pupils.

If the food industry can be convinced of the market, it will develop foods which are a positive part of a healthy eating pattern, and which are popular with chil-dren. Consumer demand is an important agent for change within the competitive market model. Helping consumers exercise that power in a constructive way is a key task for health promoters. Organisations representing sectors of profes-sional and public interests have a strong collective voice. The healthy alliance at national level as well as at local level, must influence policy.

An authoritative review of the evidence supporting the need to promote healthy eating in childhood, written in a language accessible to the new decision-makers, is required. It should clarify what action might be appropriate, why it would be effective, and what implications it might have. This evidence, combined with motivation, would encourage local people to join together to have a stronger voice, and to initiate local action.

National action must protect the health interests of those too young or too weak to protect themselves. A nutrition policy that applies throughout government is required. For example, *The health of the nation* is a government-wide strategy, but departments other than the Department of Health have been slow to act. Food skills in the National Curriculum are threatened, and the school catering service undermined by the Department for Education. MAFF appears powerless to influence European policy on dairy subsidies, and unable to influence food advertising practice directed at children. While the Treasury calls for reductions in public spending, an income gap is developing which reduces the purchasing ability of those on low incomes, including their spending on food.

What progress markers are required?

The conference drew together representatives from a wide range of professional and consumer groups. The networks and wide coverage they provide between them must be used to keep track of the effects of measures which influence children's eating patterns. As decision-making is delegated from local education authorities possibly through to individual schools, it becomes more difficult to assess overall trends, and more difficult to facilitate national changes, as fewer decisions are taken at national level. With delegation must come a responsibility to monitor and evaluate delegated services. Feedback mechanisms must form part of the contract.

Decision-makers must stay in touch with the effects of their decisions. How often do advertising control bodies sit down to watch a morning of children's food advertisements? How often do parents or school governors eat school meals? Is a statement on school food included in the annual school report?

Conclusion

Diet in school-age children in the UK is a cause for considerable concern. The effect diet has on short-term and long-term health is becoming increasingly clear. Policy decisions at all levels – national and local – must be evaluated for their impact on diet and health. There are enormous long-term economic costs of ill health in lost productivity and costs to the health service.

All the organisations represented at the conference have an important role to play both in drawing attention to the issues at national level, and in facilitating change through their members at local level.

It is only with coordinated, long-term, strategic and legislative action that positive change will be achieved and real progress made towards achieving the national health strategy targets.

List of participants

Ms Sue Allerston, Mid Glamorgan Local Education Authority
Ms Amy Berkshire, Public Health Alliance
Ms Sue Bowker, Health Promotion Wales
Ms Angela Bradley, Health Promotion Agency for Northern Ireland
Ms Sue Brighouse, Child Poverty Action Group
Mr A Hedley Brown, Society of Cardiothoracic Surgeons
Mr Michael J S Burden, Royal Pharmaceutical Society of Great Britain
Mr Geoffrey Cannon, National Food Alliance
Ms Gill Cawdron, National Forum for Coronary Heart Disease Prevention
Ms Mary Cayzer, Health Visitors' Association
Dr Jo Clarkson, Health Promotion Wales
Ms Linda Convery, Family Heart Association
Mr J R Davis, Local Authority Caterers Association
Ms Sue Dibb, Food Commission
Ms Gill Fine, British Nutrition Foundation
Dr Fleur Fisher, British Medical Association
Dr Godfrey Fowler, University of Oxford
Ms Dorothy Gardner, Local Authority Caterers Association
Professor John Goodwin, National Forum for Coronary Heart Disease Prevention
Mr Terry Grant, Department for Education
Dr Allan Hackett, Liverpool John Moores University
Ms Lucy Harris, National Consumer Council
Ms Anne Heughan, North East Thames Regional Health Authority
Dr Rose Hunt, Health Education Authority
Mr Robin Jenkins, Independent Consultant
Professor Desmond Julian, formerly British Heart Foundation
Ms Suzi Leather, National Consumer Council
Mr Martin Leighfield, Institute of Human Nutrition and Brain Chemistry
Ms Helen Lightowler, National Forum for Coronary Heart Disease Prevention
Ms Lisa Love, National Forum for Coronary Heart Disease Prevention
Ms Anne Lynd-Evans, Local Authority Caterers Association
Dr Sue Martin, Department of Health

Mr John McCandless, Institution of Environmental Health Officers
Ms Diane McCrea, Consumers' Association
Ms Liz McGranahan, Association of Primary Care Facilitators
Ms Keng Mo, National Forum for Coronary Heart Disease Prevention
Dr Michael Nelson, King's College London
Dr Noel Olsen, National Forum for Coronary Heart Disease Prevention
Ms Sandra Passmore, Community Nutrition Group
Dr Elizabeth Poskitt, British Paediatric Association
Dr Vivienne Press, Department of Health
Professor Peter Quilliam, National Forum for Coronary Heart Disease Prevention
Dr Mike Rayner, Coronary Prevention Group
Mr David Rivett, Health Education Authority
Ms Nadia Robb, Camden and Islington Health Promotion
Dr Roberto Rona, United Medical and Dental School of Guy's and St Thomas's Hospital
Ms Maggie Sanderson, British Dietetic Association
Dr George Sarna, Medical Research Council
Ms June Scarborough, National Association of Teachers of Home Economics and Technology
Ms Vibeke Schelleman, British Heart Foundation
Ms Imogen Sharp, National Forum for Coronary Heart Disease Prevention
Professor Desmond Sheridan, Royal College of Physicians of London
Ms Valerie Shield, Association of Teachers and Lecturers
Mr Hadrian Southern, National Association of Governors and Managers
Ms Susan Stainton, Essex Food Services, Essex County Council
Mr Roger Taplin, Ministry of Agriculture, Fisheries and Food
Dr Sheila Turner, Institute of Education, University of London
Ms Ann Wallis, Surrey County Council
Ms Rhiannon Walters, Faculty of Public Health Medicine
Ms Heather Waring, British Heart Foundation
Mr Richard Watt, Action and Information on Sugars
Ms Fiona Wilcock, British Nutrition Foundation
Dr Jennifer Woolfe, Ministry of Agriculture, Fisheries and Food
Mr Ian Young, Health Education Board for Scotland

The diets of children in the UK are too high in fat and sugar, and too low in fibre, iron, calcium and some vitamins. A poor diet in childhood increases the risk of health problems, both now and in later life.

Food for children: Influencing choice and investing in health outlines the nutritional content of children's diets, and the short and long-term health implications. It explores the different influences on children's eating patterns, and considers ways in which children's diets could be improved, including action by government, health professionals, schools, and food providers.

The report is produced by the National Forum for Coronary Heart Disease Prevention, an alliance of over 35 national organisations concerned with reducing the risk of heart disease in the UK.

Funding assistance from the

British Heart Foundation
The heart research charity

Price £5
ISBN 1 874279 01 2